The
POWER
of
PROCLAMATION

The
POWER
of
PROCLAMATION

BY DEREK PRINCE

THE POWER OF PROCLAMATION

© 2003, 2006 Derek Prince Ministries–International

ISBN: 978-1-892283-43-6

This book was compiled from the extensive archive of Derek Prince's unpublished materials and approved by the Derek Prince Ministries editorial team.

DEREK PRINCE MINISTRIES
P.O. BOX 19501   CHARLOTTE, NC 28219   USA
WWW.DEREKPRINCE.ORG

CONTENTS

PROCLAIMING
the
WORD

Tremendous power is released through proclaiming the Word of God. Many Christians are not aware of this amazing potential that is available to them. Whether it be a situation of personal need or an international crisis that needs to be resolved, learning how to proclaim the Word of God into that situation releases God's creative power, which can utterly transform the circumstances. Every believer has both the privilege and the responsibility to proclaim God's Word.

Throughout my years of ministry, whenever my wife Ruth was with me, I would always begin my messages by making a proclamation together with her. God taught us to begin in this way and we discovered that proclaiming the Word in faith at the beginning of a meeting makes a tremendous difference in the spiritual atmosphere in the meeting and to the anointing on the speaker.

One of my favorite proclamations is one we used frequently and in many ways sums up the message of this book.

> For as the rain comes down, and the snow from heaven, and do not return there, but water the earth, and make it bring forth and bud, that it may give seed to the sower and bread to the eater, so shall My word be that goes forth from My mouth; it shall not return to Me void, but it shall accomplish what I please, and it shall prosper in the thing for which I sent it.   Isaiah 55:10–11

What It Means to Proclaim

The word proclaim is a strong word. It comes from a Latin word that means to "shout forth." A word that is related to proclaim in the language of the New Testament is "to confess." Confession means to "say the same as." For us, as believers in the Bible, confession means that we say the same with our mouths as God has already said in His Word. We make the words of our mouth agree with the Word of God. In that way, we line ourselves up to receive the full backing and authority of Jesus.

In Hebrews 3:1 the writer says that Jesus is the "High Priest of our confession." This is a very important statement. If you have no confession, that means you have no High Priest. Jesus is our High Priest of what we confess. In other words, whenever we say with our mouths what the Bible says about us as believers in Jesus, then we have Jesus as our High Priest in heaven, releasing His authority and His blessing.

However, if we remain silent, in a certain sense, we cut off His ministry to us as High Priest. If we make a wrong confession, we do even worse. In a certain sense, we invite negative forces to surround us and move in upon us.

Proclamation is a confession that is made aggressive. It is a word that speaks of spiritual warfare. It is releasing the authority of God's Word into a situation: into your own life, the life of your church, a political situation, or whatever it may be. There are countless situations that need the power of God released into them. There is no more effective way to release the power of God than by proclamation.

Proclaiming is really the activity of a herald. Herald is a word we don't use very much today, but in medieval times a herald was a person with authority from a king or a duke or some other nobleman, who would go to a public place and make a proclamation of the will and decision of the ruler. He would shout out, "O yez, O yez!" and then make the proclamation. So whenever people heard "O yez, O yez," they knew it was the voice of authority. They would stand at attention and listen to what was being said. In the New Testament, although it doesn't clearly come out in most translations, the word preach is the word for a herald. It means "to proclaim."

Multiplying the Power of Communication

These days, through the use of modern communications technology, we can proclaim God's Word far more widely than was ever possible. I have been a Bible teacher for more than fifty years and I always felt my duty was to interpret the Bible, explain it and help people understand it.

More than twenty years ago, the Lord began to impress upon me the word proclaim. I felt that He was challenging me to go beyond teaching and begin to proclaim. The result was the beginning of my radio Bible teaching ministry, which started on eight stations in the U.S.A. in 1979 and is now translated in more than thirteen languages and effectively covers most of the globe.

Essentially it is a ministry of proclamation. The key verse that stirred me to establish the radio ministry was Matthew 24:14:

> This gospel of the kingdom will be preached in all the world as a witness to all the nations, and then the end will come.

The age cannot close until we have done our job as the church of Jesus Christ, as His witnesses on the earth. Our task is to proclaim the gospel in all the world as a witness to all the nations.

I have learned by experience the tremendous power of the Word of God simply proclaimed in faith. It accomplishes the most marvelous things. I remember the story of an American woman who was everything a woman shouldn't be by Christian standards. She was a Marxist, a feminist and a lesbian. She found herself in a small ship in the South China Sea with some of her evil companions and a storm was coming up. The others said, "Go down below, turn on the radio and see what you can find out about the weather."

She turned on the radio and just happened to catch my radio program, which was being broadcast from Manila in the Philippines. She heard enough to get saved right there and then. She is now totally different; just as radical the other way—radical for God. It was not teaching that she heard, it was simply the Word proclaimed that did its work.

The Rod of Moses

Look at the example of Moses when God called him to go back and be the deliverer of Israel out of Egypt. You remember that God appeared to him in the burning bush and then God said to him in Exodus 4 that He was sending Moses back to deliver Israel. Moses had lost all the self-confidence that he had had at the age of forty (he was now eighty). He said, "Why me, Lord? I can't do anything. How can I do it?"

In His ever-practical way, God said to Moses, "What is that in your hand?" Moses said that it was a rod, just like every shepherd of the time would carry. He didn't think there was anything particularly special about his rod. But the Lord said, "Throw it on the ground!" When he did, it became a snake and Moses ran away from his own rod. In other words, there was a potential in that rod that he had never anticipated or imagined.

Then the Lord said, "Pick it up by the tail." Everyone who deals with snakes will tell you that you should never pick a snake up that way. But Moses obeyed God and the snake became a rod once again. God said to him, in effect, "Now go with your rod. It is all you will need. You can do the whole job with that one rod." (See Exodus 3 and 4.)

If you analyze the rest of the book of Exodus from there on, the entire deliverance of Israel out of Egypt was achieved by that rod. Every time Moses wanted God to intervene, Moses stretched out his rod and God intervened. The result was that Moses wrested the rulership of Egypt out of the hand of pharaoh. That authority was symbolized by the rod in his hand. When the waters needed to be divided, at the passing through the waters of the Red Sea, Moses stretched out his rod and the waters split apart.

When the Egyptians were crossing the seabed in pursuit of the children of Israel, Moses put forth his rod again and the waters swallowed them up. The only thing Moses needed for the entire task that God had called him to was that one shepherd's rod; the very thing he didn't think had any significance when he first held it in his hand.

The Word and the Spirit Together

I want to suggest to you, if you are a Bible-believing, committed Christian, you also have a rod in your hand. It is the Word of God. Think of your Bible as the only instrument you need in your hand to be able to do everything God calls you to do.

The first thing we need to realize is the power of God's Word. It is a supernatural book. Just like Moses' rod, it contains power that isn't obvious when you first look at it. But when you begin to understand it, the power is actually limitless.

Let me give you a few Scriptures that reveal the power of the Word of God:

> By the word of the LORD were the heavens made; and all the
> host of them by the breath of his mouth.
>
> Psalm 33:6 KJV

The Hebrew word for "breath" is ruach, which is the normal word for "spirit." So all of creation took place through two agents: the Word of God and the Spirit of God. Everything that exists, has existed or will exist owes its origin to these two forces working together. The Word must work with the Spirit. I think that might be why the psalmist translated it breath and not spirit.

Think about the tremendous power of words and yet how simple they are. When I was teaching English as a second language to African students, I had to learn elementary phonetics. I discovered some interesting things about words. How do we actually speak? We release breath out of our lungs, it passes through the mouth and nose, and the various things it is subjected to determine the sound of the words that come out.

The basic truth is that you cannot speak without breathing. This is a picture of how God speaks too. Every time He speaks a word, it is carried by His breath; His Spirit. The Word and the Spirit of God always go together. The Word and the Spirit of God brought the universe into being and they sustain it as well.

There is a very powerful Scripture in 2 Peter that tells us three things: the Word creates, the Word maintains, and the Word abolishes.

By the word of God the heavens were of old, and the earth standing out of water and in the water, by which the world that then existed perished, being flooded with water. But the heavens and the earth which are now preserved by the same word, are reserved for fire until the day of judgment and perdition of ungodly men. 2 Peter 3:5–7

So by the Word of God the heavens were brought into being, by the Word of God they are maintained in being, and by the Word of God, when God's time comes, the heavens will pass away. The Word of God creates, maintains and abolishes. Sometimes, when I look at the mess that man is making of this planet, I am glad that the Word of God can abolish that mess one day. All these things God accomplishes by His Word.

Let us go back to the Scripture quoted at the beginning, Isaiah 55:10–11. This word must come out of God's mouth, otherwise it is not effective.

For as the rain comes down, and the snow from heaven, and do not return there, but water the earth, and make it bring forth and bud, that it may give seed to the sower and bread to the eater, so shall My word be that goes forth from My mouth; it shall not return to me void, but it shall accomplish what I please, and it shall prosper in the thing for which I sent it.

Notice that God said, "My word . . . that goes forth from My mouth." In other words, "My word, when it is propelled by My breath."

In 2 Corinthians 3:6 Paul says, "The letter kills." In other words, the Word by itself without the breath does not bring life. It has to be the Word and the Spirit together. You may have a sermon that has a lot of Scripture in it, but if it does not have the breath of the Spirit then it is dry. It doesn't produce life; it produces death. The two must always operate together.

I want to draw a parallel with the experience of Moses to see how we can make the Word of God effective by proclaiming it. By proclaiming it I mean releasing it into a situation. It takes confidence and boldness. It is not for the timid; you must make up your mind that you believe it.

It is God's Word, and if you say it with a believing heart through believing lips, it is just as effective as if God Himself says it when His Spirit says it through you. It doesn't have to be God Himself speaking. If the Spirit of God propels the Word of God through your mouth, it is as effective as when God spoke the universe into being.

Learning to Tremble at God's Word

The first thing that happened to Moses was that he got frightened. He threw his rod down on the ground, it became a snake and he ran from it. Before we can be effective in proclaiming, we have to learn to be afraid of the Word of God. We have to learn to tremble at the Word of God.

> Thus says the LORD:
> "Heaven is My throne,
> And earth is My footstool.
> Where is the house that you will build Me?
> And where is the place of My rest?
> For all those things My hand has made,
> And all those things exist,"
> Says the LORD.
> "But on this one will I look:
> On him who is poor and of a contrite spirit,
> And who trembles at My word."   Isaiah 66:1–2

God says that we can't build anything that will impress Him because He has already created the entire universe. But He says that there is one thing that does attract His favor: "On this one will I look [esteem or respect]."

Whom will God respect and take into account? "Him who is poor and of a contrite spirit and who trembles at My word."

So, like Moses, our first reaction has to be fear and awe at the Word of God. There is far too little fear of the Word of God in the church today. We are too familiar with it. We quote it and bandy it about, but we don't show true reverence for it. We have to change that attitude.

Let me give you two reasons from the gospel of John why we should tremble before the Word of God. The first is in John 12:47–48 where Jesus says:

> "If anyone hears My words and does not believe [receive them], I do not judge him; for I did not come to judge the world but to save the world. He who rejects Me, and does not receive My words, has that which judges him—the word that I have spoken will judge him in the last day."

We are all going to be judged by the Word of God. Imagine yourself standing before almighty God, having to give an account for your life, as I believe all of us will have to do one day. I think you would tremble; you would be very concerned. Jesus is saying that we should have the same attitude toward the Word of God because it will be the Word of God that will be our judge. Every time we open the pages of the Bible and read it, if we can understand this, we are looking at that which will one day judge us. No wonder we should tremble at it.

Then in John 14:23 Jesus makes another amazing statement:

"If anyone loves Me, he will keep My word; and My Father will love him, and We will come to him and make Our home with him."

This is one of the very few places in the Bible where the plural pronoun is used about God. "We [Father and Son] will come to him." How will we come? Through His Word. In other words, when we open up to the Word of God, then God Himself—the Father and the Son—is coming into our lives, willing to make His home with us.

If it should ever be somehow, even in a vision, you were to see the Lord Jesus coming into your home, you would be overwhelmed. You would have a sense of awe. You would want to fall at His feet. Jesus is saying here, "Not only will I come, but the Father will come as well." They will come through the Word of God.

Most of us in the contemporary church need to change our attitude towards God's Word. We need to show a greater reverence, awe, and fear. The Word won't be effective in our lives in the way that I have described until we learn to reverence that Word.

Taking Hold of God's Word

This trembling at the Word is the first thing that happened to Moses. He suddenly realized the power that was in his rod and he ran from it. He was overawed. The second thing that he did was to take hold of the rod. By faith he gripped it, and it became a rod again in his hand. So when we have trembled, then we need to take hold of God's Word.

The last few verses of Psalm 149 speak powerfully to this.

> Let the saints be joyful in glory
> Let them sing aloud on their beds.
> Let the high praises of God be in their mouth,
> And a two-edged sword in their hand;
> To execute vengeance on the nations,
> And punishments on the peoples;
> To bind their kings with chains,
> And their nobles with fetters of iron;
> To execute on them the written judgment—
> This honor have all His saints.   Psalm 149:5–9

The saints spoken of here are all true, dedicated believers, ones who tremble at the sound of the Word of God and are totally committed to it. And there is an amazing series of statements given. Can you identify yourself as belonging to the saints? If we have the high praises of God in our mouth and a two-edged sword in our hands, then we can execute judgment on the nations. Can you begin to see yourself, by faith, as part of this scenario? This honor or privilege belongs to all the saints. What an awesome responsibility. I think the way each of us prays would be quite different if we were to really see ourselves in the light of these verses.

Notice that it says "to execute . . . the written judgment." Where is that judgment written? It is in the Word. We are not the ones to make those judgments; God has made them. But we have the privilege of executing those judgments on the nations and their rulers. In other words, believers have a unique and important part to play in history.

The tragedy is that so many Christians are so far from understanding all that God has made available to us, not to mention all that God expects from us. I want to emphasize that we don't make the judgments; we find the judgments in the written Word of God. Our role is to execute them.

How do we do this? We do it by proclaiming from the Word of God the judgments that are already written there. We simply proclaim them; we are the heralds. We stand in the marketplace of the world and shout out, "O yez, O yez!" Then we announce the decree of God.

Exercising Authority

As we come to the next stage, I want to be very practical and down-to-earth. After he had grasped the rod, what did Moses do next? When he got back to Egypt, he stretched out his rod. He exercised the authority that was in the rod. I want to suggest that we need to do the same. We need to take the written Word of God and we need to stretch it out in any situation where the authority of God is needed.

One of the most effective ways to release the power of God into a situation is by proclaiming it in faith and under the anointing of the Holy Spirit. Remember that the Word must go with the breath. When the breath or Spirit of God propels His Word from out of our mouths, we can release it into a situation, and those words have all the authority of almighty God in that situation.

God did not step down off His throne, take the rod from Moses and say, "I'll do it for you." That seems to be what most of us expect to happen. But God says, "You've got the rod; you do it!" It is actually called "the rod of God" in Exodus 4:20, but Moses was still the one who held it and wielded it.

I am going to address a number of situations that need the rod of God. I will begin with matters that are personal and then move on to the regional, national and international. I want to show you different ways we can stretch out the rod. These will all be proclamations that I use regularly in my devotional times with the Lord. These times are often anything but quiet times! I'm not saying that there is more power if you shout; it all depends on how the Holy Spirit leads you at the time. I have between one and two hundred proclamations that I make on a regular basis. Some of these I have proclaimed hundreds of times.

Overcoming Negative Thinking

Remember—especially those of you who have a lot of negative thinking and speaking in your background—just saying one of these proclamations once is not going to have very much impact. They need to be spoken out loud over and over for there to come real change in the heavenly realm. You need to go on speaking these out until they become part of your thinking.

Most of you will know that my background is British and that British people can tend to be pretty negative; they are pessimists by nature. I myself was a pessimist of the pessimists! God has been gradually revolutionizing me. It has taken Him a long while!

Whenever I am in a difficult situation I automatically begin to think of all the trouble, all the bad things that could happen. Maybe you have the same problem.

I have been using the weapon of the Word in many different ways. In Jeremiah 29:11 God says to Israel:

> "I know the plans that I have for you; plans for good and not for evil." (NAS, TLB)

Other translations say, "plans to prosper you" (NIV) and "not for calamity, to give you a future and a hope" (NAS).

Every time I find myself beginning to entertain some negative picture or thought, I say, "Lord, I thank You that I know the plans You have for me; plans of good and not of evil, plans of prosperity and not of calamity, to give me a future and a hope."

I may have to say it several times, but in the end the negative atmosphere has been dissipated and I have a strong, confident, positive attitude. If you start to say that at the beginning of the day you will have a good day; you will accomplish the things that you set out to do.

Your attitude makes a huge difference in the way other people treat you. If you walk into a store with a positive attitude, the staff will help you. If you go in expecting bad service, discourtesy or trouble, that is probably what you will get.

I think it is always good to personalize the proclamations that you make. So where the Bible says "you" say "I" instead. By doing this you are saying, "This applies to me." Let's start with self-defense. I am tired of moving in the area of need; some Christians never get beyond their own needs.

Suppose you are attacked by a lot of fearful, negative thoughts and you find yourself continually thinking about what would happen if you were to die. Perhaps you need surgery and the doctor says that he can't guarantee you will come through it.

Ruth and I faced this together when she was ill. Here is a Scripture we must have used thousands of times:

> I shall not die, but live,
> And declare the works of the LORD.   Psalm 118:17

Protection through Proclamation

Suppose people are speaking or even praying against you. Your remedy is Isaiah 54:17:

> No weapon that is formed against us shall prosper,
> And every tongue that rises against us in judgment we do
>   condemn.
> This is our heritage as servants of the LORD,
> And our righteousness is from You, O LORD of Hosts.

Ruth and I used to say this every night before going to sleep. When we confess that our righteousness is from the Lord, this is the reason we can condemn the tongues that accuse us. It is because they are refusing God's righteousness and that always means being on the losing side.

I would like to make clear, too, that we would say, "If there are those who speak against us or are seeking evil for us, we forgive them. And having forgiven them, we bless them in the name of the Lord." We always seek to replace the negative with the positive.

The Bible says that if people curse us we should not curse them back but rather bless them. Paul said, "Do not be overcome by evil, but overcome evil with good" (Romans 12:21). Goodness is the only power strong enough to overcome evil.

If our ministry is attacked, we use a proclamation from Deuteronomy 33:25–27:

> The bolts of our gates will be iron and bronze,
> and our strength will equal our days.
> There is no one like the God of Jeshurun,
> who rides on the heavens to help us
> and on the clouds in his majesty.
> The eternal God is our refuge,
> and underneath are the everlasting arms.
> He will drive out our enemy before us saying, "Destroy
> him!"
> (NIV)

That kind of proclamation really frightens Satan. Remember that our battle is not against flesh and blood but against spiritual powers of wickedness in heavenly realms. The weapons God provides are very powerful, but they must be used in the right context.

Financial and Physical Needs

You may have various kinds of need; financial or physical for instance. For financial needs we use 2 Corinthians 9:8. We have changed the words a little, but basically it is from the King James Version:

God is able to make all grace abound toward us, that we, always having all sufficiency in all things, may abound in every good work.

It all starts with three simple words: "God is able." Then it says what He is able to do. In this amazing verse the word all occurs five times and the word abound occurs twice. It would hardly be possible to get more abundance into one verse! It is all grace. And how is grace received? "By grace you have been saved through faith" (Ephesians 2:8). It is not something we earn or deserve. It does not depend on our social standing. We receive everything by faith in God's grace. This verse is the financial foundation of our ministry.

Then, suppose you are faced with something challenging that you think you can't do. You feel that you don't have the education, the physical strength, the discernment—whatever it is that the situation requires. In such circumstances we resort to Philippians 4:13. This is the "Prince version." I know Greek, and I think the Lord has given me a really good rendering of the Greek that brings out the meaning better than any other version I know of:

I can do all things through the one who empowers me within.

I use the word empower because the Greek word is from dunamis, which is normally translated "power." So, there is a source of power within you that is released by your proclamation. Even if I don't have the education, the strength or the discernment to do something, when it is a task assigned by the will of God, there is One in me who empowers me from within.

You may be afflicted by sickness of some kind. One of our favorite verses dealing with healing is 1 Peter 2:24:

Jesus Himself bore our sins in His own body on the tree,
that we, having died to sins, might live for righteousness—
by whose wounds we were healed.

Notice, it is expressed in the past tense. When the Bible speaks about healing in the atonement, the future tense is never used. Seven hundred years before Jesus came, Isaiah said, "By His stripes we are healed" (Isaiah 53:5). After the atonement, looking back, Peter said, "By whose wounds we were healed."

That gives you a totally different perspective. It doesn't mean that you automatically cease to be sick, but it gives you a different basis on which to encounter and challenge sickness.

Sometimes you will have to keep confessing it for a long time. You just have to decide which is more reliable—God's Word or your symptoms?

Proclamation in National and International Affairs

Now, to move to an area where a more aggressive approach is necessary. I want to deal with intervention in national and international affairs. Ruth and I used to spend a lot of time praying outside our own personal needs for all kinds of situations, including the destiny of nations. Here are some Scriptures that will encourage and help you.

One of our favorites is a combination of Daniel 2:20–22 and Daniel 4:34–35. The first words were spoken by Daniel and the second by Nebuchadnezzar, but the message is the same.

> Blessed be the name of God for ever and ever,
> For wisdom and might are His.
> And He changes the times and the seasons,
> He removes kings and raises up kings,
> He gives wisdom to the wise
> And knowledge to those who have understanding.
> He reveals deep and secret things;
> He knows what is in the darkness,
> And the light dwells with Him.
> For His dominion is an everlasting dominion,
> And His kingdom is from generation to generation.
> All the inhabitants of the earth are reputed as nothing;
> He does according to His will in the army of heaven
> And among the inhabitants of the earth.
> No one can restrain His hand or say to Him, "What have
> You done?"

Remember that the second section of those words came from a ruler who not long before that had been an unbeliever. That should encourage us that God can indeed change the hearts of evil rulers if we learn how to pray.

Then there are two passages from 2 Chronicles. They are both single verse prayers and we often speak these out to get us going before we focus on praying more for the specific aspects of the particular situation at hand. The first is in 2 Chronicles 14:11:

LORD, there is no one like you to help the powerless against the mighty. Help us, O LORD our God, for we rely on you, and in your name we have come against this vast army. O LORD, you are our God; do not let man prevail against you.

(NIV)

The second one is 2 Chronicles 20:6:

O LORD, God of our fathers, are you not the God who is in heaven? You rule over all the kingdoms of the earth. Power and might are in your hand, and no one can withstand you.

(NIV)

Now look at Psalm 33:8–12, which is a tremendously powerful affirmation when you are dealing with the world situation:

Let all the earth fear the LORD,
Let all the inhabitants of the world stand in awe of Him,
For He spoke, and it was done,
He commanded, and it stood fast.
The LORD brings the counsel of the nations to nothing;
He makes the plans of the peoples of no effect.
The counsel of the LORD stands forever,
The plans of His heart to all generations.
Blessed is the nation whose God is the LORD,
And the people He has chosen as His own inheritance.

In other words, who is going to come out of it all as a winner?

The nation whose God is the Lord. All the plans of governments, nations, the United Nations, and so on, are just nonsense if they are contrary to the plan of God.

Concerning Christianity and Opposing Forces

Finally, I want to look at some verses that relate specifically to Israel, which is one of the areas we have most prayed about over the years. You may not have exactly the same burden, but you can take the principles and apply them in your particular situation.

The regions of the world that are now often referred to as the 10/40 Window have proven to be among the hardest to penetrate with the truth of the gospel. I believe there is a very important reason for this that actually underlines the impact that proclamation can have.

You probably know that five times a day, every day, from every Muslim mosque in the world, the proclamation goes forth, "There is no God but Allah, and Mohammed is his prophet." This proclamation has been going out every day for more than 1400 years. You don't have to do the calculation to realize that this proclamation has gone out billions of times over the centuries.

It helps us understand why there is such a tremendously strong power over that whole region. What is the cause of this? I believe it has much to do with the power of that proclamation.

The principle applies no matter whether the proclamation is positive or negative. In order to overcome the accumulated power of negative proclamations, we have to make positive proclamations to counter them.

If you think that this is a hopeless task, remember the situation when Moses was confronted by the Egyptian magicians. When they all threw their rods on the ground and the rods became snakes, Moses' snake ate up the snakes of the Egyptian magicians. Our proclamation can overcome every negative proclamation if we know how to make it.

Now I want to look at two biblical proclamations specifically in regard to Israel and her land. The first is from Psalm 125:3:

> The scepter of the wicked will not remain over the land allotted to the righteous. (NIV)

In this context, the "scepter of the wicked" is represented by any force that is opposed to Christianity. You will have to speak out this verse in faith, especially when everything looks exactly the opposite. Actually, that's the best time to say it! You are stretching out your rod of authority, and your rod (or snake) is going to eat up all the snakes of the magicians.

The second proclamation regarding Israel is in Psalm 129:5–6:

> Let them all be confounded and turned back that hate Zion. Let them be like the grass upon the housetops, which withers before it grows up. (KJV)

I serve notice on all those who hate Zion that they will never grow to full maturity; they will wither before they are fully grown. That is the Word of God, and it is going to come to pass.

Let me give you one more passage about the restoration of Israel in Jeremiah 31:7:

> Sing with gladness for Jacob,
> And shout among the chief of the nations;
> Proclaim, give praise, and say,
> "O LORD, save Your people,
> The remnant of Israel!"

Look at the verbs in that verse: sing, shout, proclaim, praise and pray. These are all specific actions that we can be involved in. The word proclaim is right in there as well. Then it says in verse 10:

> Hear the word of the LORD, O nations,
> And declare it in the isles afar off, and say,
> "He who scattered Israel will gather him,
> And will keep him as a shepherd keeps his flock."

This is something we can proclaim or declare over all the nations, especially those in the 10/40 Window. The same God who scattered Israel is now gathering them once again. As God's people, we can have a part to play in proclaiming the truth of God's Word until it becomes a reality.

Practical Application

Now I want to share with you many of the proclamations that Ruth and I used both publicly and privately over the twenty years of our marriage.

These proclamations are arranged by category to help you use them appropriately. There are more than a hundred of them. So if you wanted to use one every day there would be enough for four months, then you could start all over again.

As an example, here is a combination of proclamations entitled A Declaration of Confidence in God's Protection. I make this proclamation on a regular basis and have found it to be of tremendous benefit in my life.

Many testimonies have been received over the years from people sharing how they have been set free and have experienced a greater sense of God's presence as they have proclaimed the truths contained in this proclamation.

I encourage you to take this proclamation and all the other ones in this book, meditate on them and apply them in faith to your life. You could use them when you get up in the morning and before you go to sleep at night.

I believe it is more effective to actually speak them out loud rather than just read them. It is good to repeat the proclamation a number of times to enable it to sink into your spirit.

Declaration of Confidence in God's Protection

No weapon that is formed against me shall prosper and every tongue that arises against me in judgment I do condemn. This is my heritage as a servant of the LORD and my righteousness is from You, O LORD of Hosts.

If there are those who have been speaking or praying against me, or seeking to harm me, or who have rejected me, I forgive them (name people if you know them). Having forgiven them, I bless them in the name of the LORD.[1]

Now I declare, O LORD, that You and You alone are my

God and beside You there is no other; a just God and a Savior, the Father, the Son and the Spirit, and I worship You!

I submit myself afresh to You today in unreserved obedience. Having submitted to You, LORD, I do as Your Word directs. I resist the devil: all his pressures, his attacks, his deceptions and every instrument or agent he would seek to use against me. I do not submit! I resist him, drive him from me and exclude him from me in the name of Jesus.

Specifically I reject and repel: infirmity, infection, pain, inflammation, malignancies, allergies, viruses, _____,[2] every form of witchcraft and every type of stress.

Finally, LORD, I thank You that through the sacrifice of Jesus on the cross, I have passed out from under the curse and entered into the blessing of Abraham whom You blessed in all things: exaltation, health, reproductiveness, prosperity, victory, God's favor and God's friendship.[3]

Amen

The following scriptural proclamations have been tested and tried in our own experience. The passages we have memorized have been taken from the particular version that the Holy Spirit has made alive to us. Where we have felt it appropriate to make significant changes in the wording, this has been indicated by an asterisk (*).

Categories for Proclamations

The Scriptures have been grouped under the following categories:

> Fear of the Lord
>
> Righteousness and Holiness
>
> Health and Strength
>
> Guidance, Protection, Preservation
>
> God's Intervention in Human Affairs
>
> Testing and Trials
>
> Spiritual Conflict
>
> Perfect Redemption
>
> Mental and Emotional Stability
>
> Serving God

Finally, at the end, there are three comprehensive proclamations which are special favorites of mine.

After a while, you will probably find other Scriptures that the Holy Spirit makes alive for you in a special way. The pages at the end of each section are for those personal prayers and proclamations.

I pray that these Scriptures will do as much for you as they have done for us. They have made the difference between defeat and victory!

PROCLAMATIONS

FEAR
of the
LORD

The fear of the LORD, that is wisdom,
And to depart from evil is understanding.

Job 28:28

But as for me, I trust in You, O LORD;
I say, "You are my God."
My times are in Your hand.
Oh, how great is Your goodness,
Which You have laid up for us who fear You,
Which You have prepared for us who trust in You
In the presence of the sons of men!
You shall hide us in the secret place of Your presence
From the plots of man;
You shall keep us secretly in a pavilion
From the strife of tongues.

Psalm 31:14–15a, 19–20

Come, you children, listen to me;
>I will teach you the fear of the LORD.
Who is the man who desires life,
>And loves many days, that he may see good?
Keep your tongue from evil,
>And your lips from speaking guile.
Depart from evil, and do good; seek peace, and pursue it.

Psalm 34:11–14

The fear of the LORD is the beginning of wisdom;
A good understanding have all those who practice it.
His praise endures forever.

Psalm 111:10*

The fear of the LORD is the beginning of knowledge,
But fools despise wisdom and instruction.

Proverbs 1:7

The fear of the LORD is to hate evil;
Pride and arrogance and the evil way
And the perverse mouth I hate.

Proverbs 8:13

The fear of the LORD is the beginning of wisdom,
And the knowledge of the Holy One is understanding.
For by me your days will be multiplied,
And years of life will be added to you.

Proverbs 9:10–11

In the fear of the LORD there is strong confidence,
And His children will have a place of refuge.
The fear of the LORD is a fountain of life,
To avoid the snares of death.

Proverbs 14:26–27

The fear of the LORD leads to life,
And he who has it will abide in satisfaction;
He will not be visited with evil.

Proverbs 19:23

By humility and the fear of the LORD
Are riches and honor and life.

Proverbs 22:4

Personal Prayers and Proclamations

_____

_____

_____

_____

_____

_____

_____

_____

_____

_____

_____

_____

_____

_____

_____

_____

_____

_____

_____

_____

_____

_____

_____

_____

RIGHTEOUSNESS
and
HOLINESS

Therefore we also, since we are surrounded by so great a cloud of witnesses, let us lay aside every weight, and the sin which so easily ensnares us, and let us run with endurance the race that is set before us,

looking unto Jesus, the author and perfecter of our faith, who for the joy that was set before Him endured the cross, despising the shame, and has sat down at the right hand of the throne of God.

But we have come to Mount Zion and to the city of the living God, the heavenly Jerusalem, to an innumerable company of angels in festal array,

to the church of the firstborn who are registered in heaven, to God the Judge of all, to the spirits of just men made perfect,

to Jesus the Mediator of a new covenant, and to the blood of sprinkling that speaks better things than that of Abel.   Hebrews 12:1–2, 22–24*

And this we pray, that our love may abound still more and more in knowledge and all discernment,

that we may approve the things that are excellent, that we may be sincere and without offense till the day of Christ,

being filled with the fruits of righteousness which are by Jesus Christ, to the glory and praise of God.

Philippians 1:9–11

Who can understand his errors?
Cleanse me from secret faults.
Keep back Your servant also from presumptuous sins;
Let them not have dominion over me.
Then I shall be blameless,
And I shall be innocent of great transgression.
Let the words of my mouth and the meditation of my
heart
Be acceptable in Your sight,
O LORD, my strength and my redeemer.

Psalm 19:12–14

But the hour is coming, and now is, when the true worshipers will worship the Father in spirit and truth; for the Father is seeking such to worship Him.

God is Spirit, and those who worship Him must worship in spirit and truth.

John 4:23–24

This our prayer:

that we may be filled with the knowledge of His will in all wisdom and spiritual understanding;

that we may have a walk worthy of the Lord, fully pleasing Him, being fruitful in every good work and increasing in the knowledge of God;

strengthened with all might, according to His glorious power, for all patience and longsuffering with joy;

giving thanks to the Father who has qualified us to be partakers of the inheritance of the saints in the light.

He has delivered us from the domain of darkness and translated us into the kingdom of the Son of His love,

in whom we have redemption through His blood, the forgiveness of sins.

Colossians 1:9b–14*

My son, if you receive my words,
And treasure my commands within you,
So that you incline your ear to wisdom,
And apply your heart to understanding;
Yes, if you cry out for discernment,
And lift up your voice for understanding,
If you seek her as silver,
And search for her as for hidden treasures;
Then you will understand the fear of the LORD,
And find the knowledge of God.

Proverbs 2:1–5

Now may the God of peace Himself sanctify us completely; and may our whole spirit, soul, and body be preserved blameless at the coming of our Lord Jesus Christ.

He who calls us is faithful, who also will do it.

1 Thessalonians 5:23–24

Blessed is the man
Who walks not in the counsel of the ungodly,
Nor stands in the path of sinners,
Nor sits in the seat of the scornful;
But his delight is in the law of the LORD,
And in His law he meditates day and night.
He shall be like a tree planted by the rivers of water,
That brings forth its fruit in its season,
Whose leaf also shall not wither;
And whatever he does shall prosper.

Psalm 1:1–3

Thus says the High and Lofty One
Who inhabits eternity, whose name is Holy:
    "I dwell in the high and holy place,
    With him who has a contrite and humble spirit,
    To revive the spirit of the humble,
    And to revive the heart of the contrite ones."
This is the one I esteem:
    He who is humble and contrite in spirit,
    And trembles at my word.

Isaiah 57:15; 66:2b (NIV)

As the elect of God, holy and beloved, we put on tender mercies, kindness, humbleness of mind, meekness, longsuffering;

bearing with one another, and forgiving one another, if anyone has a complaint against another; even as Christ forgave us, so we also must do.

But above all these things we put on love, which is the bond of perfection.

We let the peace of God rule in our hearts, to which also we were called in one body, and we are thankful.

We let the word of Christ dwell in us richly in all wisdom, teaching and admonishing one another in psalms and hymns and spiritual songs, singing with grace in our hearts to the Lord.

And whatever we do in word or deed, we do all in the name of the Lord Jesus, giving thanks to God the Father through Him.   Colossians 3:12–17*

The grace of God that brings salvation has appeared to all men,

teaching us that, denying ungodliness and worldly lusts, we should live soberly, righteously, and godly in this present age,

looking for the blessed hope and glorious appearing of our great God and Savior Jesus Christ,

who gave Himself for us, that He might redeem us from every lawless deed and purify for Himself His own special people, zealous for good works.

Titus 2:11–14

Beloved, let us love one another, for love is of God; and everyone who loves is born of God and knows God.

He who does not love does not know God, for God is love.

In this the love of God was manifested toward us, that God has sent His only begotten Son into the world, that we might live through Him.

In this is love, not that we loved God, but that He loved us and sent His Son to be the propitiation for our sins.

Beloved, if God so loved us, we also ought to love one another.

We have known and believed the love that God has for us. God is love, and he who abides in love abides in God, and God in him.

1 John 4:7–11, 16

Finally, there is laid up for me
　　the crown of righteousness,
　　which the Lord, the righteous Judge,
　　will give to me on that Day,
and not to me only
　　but also to all who have loved His appearing.

2 Timothy 4:8

Blessed are the poor in spirit,
> For theirs is the kingdom of heaven.

Blessed are those who mourn,
> For they shall be comforted.

Blessed are the meek,
> For they shall inherit the earth.

Blessed are those who hunger and thirst for righteousness,
> For they shall be filled.

Blessed are the merciful,
> For they shall obtain mercy.

Blessed are the pure in heart,
> For they shall see God.

Blessed are the peacemakers,
> For they shall be called sons of God.

Blessed are those who are persecuted for righteousness'
> sake,
> For theirs is the kingdom of heaven.

Blessed are you when they revile and persecute you, and say all kinds of evil against you falsely for My sake.

Rejoice and be exceedingly glad, for great is your reward in heaven, for so they persecuted the prophets who were before you.

Matthew 5:3–12

Personal Prayers and Proclamations

_____
_____
_____
_____
_____
_____
_____
_____
_____
_____
_____
_____
_____
_____
_____
_____
_____
_____
_____
_____
_____
_____
_____
_____
_____
_____

HEALTH
and
STRENGTH

Have you not known?

Have you not heard?

The everlasting God, the Lord,

The Creator of the ends of the earth,

Neither faints nor is weary.

There is no searching of His understanding.

He gives power to the weak,

And to those who have no might He increases strength.

Even the youths shall faint and be weary,

And the young men shall utterly fall,

But those who wait on the Lord

Shall renew their strength;

They shall mount up with wings like eagles,

They shall run and not be weary,

They shall walk and not faint.

Isaiah 40:28–31

God's strength is made perfect in my weakness, so when
I am weak, then I am strong.

> Based on 2 Corinthians 12:9–10

The righteous will flourish like a palm tree,
    they will grow like a cedar of Lebanon;
planted in the house of the LORD,
    they will flourish in the courts of our God.
They will still bear fruit in old age;
    they will stay fresh and green,
proclaiming, "The LORD is upright;
    He is my Rock, and there is no unrighteousness in Him."

> Psalm 92:12–15 (NIV)*

But I will hope continually,
And will praise You yet more and more.
My mouth shall tell of Your righteousness
And of Your salvation all the day,
For I do not know their limits.
I will go in the strength of the Lord GOD;
I will make mention of Your righteousness, of Yours only.
O God, You have taught me from my youth;
And to this day I declare Your wondrous works.
Now also, even if I become old and grayheaded,
O God, do not forsake me,
Until I declare Your strength to this generation,
Your power to everyone who is to come.

> Psalm 71:14–18*

My son, let them not depart from your eyes—
Keep sound wisdom and discretion;
So they will be life to your soul
And grace to your neck.
Then you will walk safely in your way,
And your foot will not stumble.
When you lie down, you will not be afraid;
Yes, you will lie down and your sleep will be sweet.
Do not be afraid of sudden terror,
Nor of trouble from the wicked when it comes;
For the Lord will be your confidence,
And will keep your foot from being caught.

Proverbs 3:21–26

I can do all things through the One who empowers me within.[4]

Philippians 4:13

The Lord will give strength to His people;
The Lord will bless His people with peace.

Psalm 29:11

O God, You are more awesome than Your holy places.
The God of Israel is He who gives strength and power to
　　　His people.
Blessed be God!

Psalm 68:35

My son, attend to my words;
    incline thine ear unto my sayings.
Let them not depart from thine eyes;
    keep them in the midst of thine heart.
For they are life unto those that find them,
    and health to all their flesh.
Keep thy heart with all diligence,
    for out of it are the issues of life.

                    Proverbs 4:20–23 (KJV)

Now the Lord is the Spirit;
    and where the Spirit of the Lord is, there is liberty.
But we all, with unveiled face,
    beholding as in a mirror the glory of the Lord,
    are being transformed into the same image from
      glory to glory,
    just as by the Spirit of the Lord.

                    2 Corinthians 3:17–18

Personal Prayers and Proclamations

GUIDANCE, PROTECTION, *and* PRESERVATION

The LORD shall preserve me from all evil;
He shall preserve my soul.
The LORD shall preserve my going out and my coming in
From this time forth, and even forevermore.

There is a path which no fowl knoweth,
    and which the vulture's eye hath not seen:
The lion's whelps have not trodden it,
    nor the fierce lion passed by it. . . .
Seeing it is hid from the eyes of all living,
    and kept close from the fowls of the air.

Psalm 121:7–8

Job 28:7–8, 21 (KJV)

The LORD is my light and my salvation;

Whom shall I fear?

The LORD is the strength of my life;

Of whom shall I be afraid?

When the wicked came against me

To eat up my flesh,

My enemies and foes,

They stumbled and fell.

Though an army should encamp against me,

My heart shall not fear;

Though war should rise against me,

In this I will be confident.

One thing I have desired of the LORD,

That will I seek:

That I may dwell in the house of the LORD

All the days of my life,

To behold the beauty of the LORD,

And to inquire in His temple.

For in the time of trouble

He shall hide me in His pavilion;

In the secret place of His tabernacle

He shall hide me;

He shall set me high upon a rock.

And now my head shall be lifted up above my enemies all
        around me;

Therefore I will offer sacrifices of joy in His tabernacle;

I will sing, yes, I will sing praises to the LORD.

                              Psalm 27:1–6

See, I am sending an angel ahead of you to guard you along the way and to bring you to the place I have prepared.

Pay attention to him and listen to what he says. Do not rebel against him; he will not forgive your rebellion, since My Name is in him.

If you listen carefully to what he says and do all that I say, I will be an enemy to your enemies and will oppose those who oppose you.

My angel will go ahead of you and bring you into the land of the Amorites, Hittites, Perizzites, Canaanites, Hivites and Jebusites, and I will wipe them out.

Do not bow down before their gods or worship them or follow their practices. You must demolish them and break their sacred stones to pieces.

Worship the Lord your God, and His blessing will be on your food and water.

I will take away sickness from among you, and no one will miscarry or be barren in your land. I will give you a full life span.

I will send my terror ahead of you and throw into confusion every nation you encounter.

I will make all your enemies turn their backs and run.

Exodus 23:20–27 (NIV)

I shall not die, but live,
And declare the works of the Lord.

Psalm 118:17

Unless the LORD builds the house,
They labor in vain that build it;
Unless the LORD guards the city,
The watchman stays awake in vain.   Psalm 127:1

We trust in the LORD with all our heart,
    And do not lean on our own understanding;
In all our ways we acknowledge Him,
    And He directs our paths.
We are not wise in our own eyes;
    We fear the LORD and depart from evil.
It will be health to our inward parts,
    And strength to our bones.

                                    Proverbs 3:5–8

    This Book of the Law shall not depart from your mouth, but you shall meditate in it day and night, that you may observe to do according to all that is written in it. For then you will make your way prosperous, and then you will have good success.

    Have I not commanded you? Be strong and of good courage; do not be afraid, nor be dismayed, for the LORD your God is with you wherever you go.

                                    Joshua 1:8–9

The LORD is good,
A stronghold in the day of trouble;
And He knows those who trust in Him.

                                    Nahum 1:7

Blessed is the man whom You instruct, O LORD,
And teach out of Your law,
That You may give him relief from the days of adversity,
Until the pit is dug for the wicked.

Psalm 94:12–13

Fear not, for I am with you;
Be not dismayed, for I am your God.
I will strengthen you,
Yes, I will help you,
I will uphold you with the right hand of My righteousness.

Isaiah 41:10*

I know the plans I have for you,
Plans of peace and not of evil,
Plans of prosperity and not of calamity,
To give you a future and a hope.

Jeremiah 29:11 (NIV)*

As for God, His way is perfect;
The word of the LORD is proven;
He is a shield to all who trust in Him.

Psalm 18:30

The Lord will deliver me from every evil work
And preserve me for His heavenly kingdom.
To Him be glory forever and ever. Amen!

2 Timothy 4:18

You pushed me violently, that I might fall,
>But the LORD helped me.
The LORD is my strength and my song,
>And He has become my salvation.
The voice of rejoicing and salvation
>Is in the tents of the righteous;
The right hand of the LORD does valiantly.
>The right hand of LORD is exalted;
>The right hand of the LORD does valiantly.
I shall not die, but live,
>And declare the works of the LORD.
The LORD has chastened me severely,
>But He has not given me over to death.

Psalm 118:13–18

Through the LORD's mercies we are not consumed,
Because His compassions fail not.
They are new every morning;
Great is Your faithfulness.
"The LORD is my portion," says my soul,
Therefore I hope in Him!"
The LORD is good to those who wait for Him,
To the soul who seeks Him.
It is good that one should hope and wait quietly
For the salvation of the LORD.

Lamentations 3:22–26

Let all those rejoice who put their trust in You;
Let them ever shout for joy,
>because You protect and defend them;
Let those also who love Your name
>Be joyful in You.
For You, O LORD, will bless the righteous;
With favor You will surround him as with a shield.

Psalm 5:11–12*

Personal Prayers and Proclamations

_____

_____

_____

_____

_____

_____

_____

_____

_____

_____

_____

_____

_____

_____

_____

_____

_____

_____

_____

_____

_____

_____

_____

_____

_____

_____

_____

_____

GOD'S INTERVENTION
in
HUMAN AFFAIRS

Blessed be the name of God forever and ever,
For wisdom and might are His.
And He changes the times and the seasons;
He removes kings and raises up kings;
He gives wisdom to the wise
And knowledge to those who have understanding.
He reveals deep and secret things;
He knows what is in the darkness,
And the light dwells with Him. . . .

For His dominion is an everlasting dominion,
And His kingdom is from generation to generation.
All the inhabitants of the earth are reputed as nothing;
He does according to His will in the army of heaven
And among the inhabitants of the earth.
No one can restrain His hand
Or say to Him, "What have You done?"

Daniel 2:20–22, 4:34–35

For by grace we have been saved through faith, and that not of ourselves; it is the gift of God, not of works, lest anyone should boast.

For we are God's workmanship, created in Christ Jesus for good works, which God prepared beforehand that we should walk in them.

Ephesians 2:8–10

Show Your marvelous lovingkindness by Your right hand,
O You who save those who trust in You
From those who rise up against them.
Keep me as the apple of Your eye;
Hide me in the shadow of Your wings,
From the wicked who oppress me,
From my deadly enemies who surround me.

Psalm 17:7–9

Lord, there is no one like you to help the powerless against the mighty. Help us, O Lord our God, for we rely on you, and in your name we have come against this vast army. O Lord, you are our God; do not let man prevail against you.

2 Chronicles 14:11 (NIV)

O Lord, God of our fathers, are you not the God who is in
        heaven?
You rule over all the kingdoms of the nations,
Power and might are in your hand, and no one can
        withstand you.   2 Chronicles 20:6 (NIV)

We remember the prisoners as if chained with them,
    and those who are mistreated,
    since we ourselves are in the body also.

Hebrews 13:3

And to the angel of the church in Philadelphia write,
'These things says He who is holy, He who is true,
He who has the key of David,
He who opens and no one shuts,
and shuts and no one opens":
    I know your works.
    See, I have set before you an open door,
    and no one can shut it;
    for you have a little strength,
    have kept My word,
    and have not denied My name.

Revelation 3:7–8

Let them all be confounded and turned back that hate
        Zion.
Let them be as the grass upon the housetops,
    which withers before it grows up.

Psalm 129:5–6 (KJV)

Destroy, O LORD, and confound their tongues . . .

Psalm 55:9

The scepter of the wicked will not remain over the
land allotted to the righteous.

Psalm 125:3 (NIV)

Seek the LORD,
    all you meek of the earth,
    Who have upheld His justice.
Seek righteousness, seek humility.
It may be that you will be hidden
    In the day of the LORD's anger.

Zephaniah 2:3

For the LORD will not forsake His people,
    for His great name's sake,
Because it has pleased the LORD
    to make Israel His people.

1 Samuel 12:22*

"Remember Abraham, Isaac, and Israel, Your servants,
to whom You swore by Your own self, and said to them, 'I
will multiply your descendants as the stars of heaven; and
all this land that I have spoken of I give to your descendants, and they shall inherit it forever.'"

Exodus 32:13

Let all the earth fear the Lord;

Let all the inhabitants of the world stand in awe of Him.

For He spoke, and it was done;

He commanded, and it stood fast.

The Lord brings the counsel of the nations to nothing;

He makes the plans of the peoples of no effect.

The counsel of the Lord stands forever,

The plans of His heart to all generations.

Blessed is the nation whose God is the Lord,

And the people whom He chose as His own inheritance.

Psalm 33:8–12

"If it had not been the Lord who was on our side,"

    Let Israel now say—

"If it had not been the Lord who was on our side,

When men rose up against us,

Then would have swallowed us alive,

When their wrath was kindled against us;

    Then the waters would have overwhelmed us,

    The stream would have swept over our soul;

    Then the swollen waters would have swept over our soul."

Blessed be the Lord,

    Who has not given us as prey to their teeth.

Our soul has escaped as a bird from the snare of the fowlers;

The snare is broken, and we have escaped.

Our help is in the name of the Lord,

    Who made heaven and earth.

Psalm 124

Pray for the peace of Jerusalem:
"May they prosper who love you.
Peace be within your walls,
    prosperity within your palaces."

Psalm 122:6–7

Personal Prayers and Proclamations

_____

_____

_____

_____

_____

_____

_____

_____

_____

_____

_____

_____

_____

_____

_____

_____

_____

_____

_____

_____

_____

_____

_____

_____

_____

_____

TESTING
and
TRIALS

But thanks be to God, who gives us the victory through our Lord Jesus Christ.

Therefore, my beloved brethren, we are steadfast, immovable, always abounding in the work of the Lord, knowing that our labor is not in vain in the Lord.

1 Corinthians 15:57–58

I will bless the LORD at all times;
His praise shall continually be in my mouth.
My soul shall make its boast in the LORD;
The humble shall hear of it and be glad.
Oh, magnify the LORD with me,
And let us exalt His name together.
I sought the LORD, and He heard me,
And delivered me from all my fears.

Psalm 34:1–4

Therefore we submit to God.

We resist the devil and he will flee from us.

James 4:7

Therefore I endure all things for the sake of the elect, that they also may obtain the salvation which is in Christ Jesus with eternal glory.

This is a faithful saying:

For if we died with Him,

We shall also live with Him.

If we endure,

We shall also reign with Him.

If we deny Him,

He also will deny us.

If we are faithless,

He remains faithful;

He cannot deny Himself.

2 Timothy 2:10–13

We count it all joy, when we fall into various trials,

knowing that the testing of our faith produces

endurance.

But we let endurance have its perfect work,

that we may be perfect and complete,

lacking nothing.

James 1:2–4*

Blessed be the God and Father of our Lord Jesus Christ, who according to His abundant mercy has begotten us again to a living hope through the resurrection of Jesus Christ from the dead,

to an inheritance incorruptible and undefiled and that does not fade away, reserved in heaven for us,

who are kept by the power of God through faith for salvation ready to be revealed in the last time.

In this we greatly rejoice, though now for a little while, if need be, we have been distressed by various trials,

that the genuineness of our faith, being much more precious than gold that perishes, though it is tested by fire, may be found to praise, honor, and glory at the revelation of Jesus Christ, whom having not seen we love.

Though now we do not see Him, yet believing, we rejoice with joy inexpressible and full of glory,

receiving the end of our faith—the salvation of our souls.

1 Peter 1:3–9

Blessed is the man who trusts in the LORD,
And whose hope is in the LORD.
For he shall be like a tree planted by the waters,
Which spreads out its roots by the river,
And will not fear when heat comes;
But its leaf will be green,
And will not be anxious in the year of drought,
Nor will cease from yielding fruit.

Jeremiah 17:7–8

If God is for us, who can be against us?

He who did not spare His own Son, but delivered Him up for us all, how shall He not with Him also freely give us all things?

Who shall bring a charge against God's elect? It is God who justifies.

Who is he who condemns? It is Christ who died, and furthermore is also risen, who is even at the right hand of God, who also makes intercession for us.

Who shall separate us from the love of Christ?

Shall tribulation, or distress,

Or persecution, or famine,

Or nakedness, or peril, or sword?

As it is written:

"For Your sake we are killed all day long;

We are accounted as sheep for the slaughter."

Yet in all these things we are more than conquerors through Him who loved us.

For I am persuaded that neither death nor life,

Nor angels nor principalities nor powers,

Nor things present nor things to come,

Nor height nor depth, nor any other created thing,

shall be able to separate us from the love of God which is in Christ Jesus our Lord.

Romans 8:31b–39

Personal Prayers and Proclamations

_____

_____

_____

_____

_____

_____

_____

_____

_____

_____

_____

_____

_____

_____

_____

_____

_____

_____

_____

_____

_____

_____

SPIRITUAL CONFLICT

God resists the proud,

But gives grace to the humble.

Therefore we humble ourselves under the mighty hand of God, that He may exalt us in due time,

having cast all our care upon Him, for He cares for us.

We are sober, we are vigilant; because our adversary the devil walks about like a roaring lion, seeking whom he may devour.

We resist him, steadfast in the faith, knowing that the same sufferings are experienced by our brotherhood in the world.

But the God of all grace, who called us to His eternal glory by Christ Jesus, after we have suffered a while, will perfect, establish, strengthen, and settle us.

To Him be the glory and the dominion forever and ever. Amen.

1 Peter 5:5b–11*

For though we walk in the flesh, we do not war after the flesh:

for the weapons of our warfare are not carnal, but mighty through God to the pulling down of strongholds;

casting down imaginations, and every high thing that exalteth itself against the knowledge of God, and bringing into captivity every thought to the obedience of Christ.

2 Corinthians 10:3–5 (KJV)

We overcome Satan by the blood of the Lamb
and by the word of our testimony,
and we do not love our lives to the death.

Revelation 12:11

The bolts of our gates will be iron and bronze,
and our strength will equal our days.
There is no one like the God of Jeshurun,
who rides on the heavens to help us
and on the clouds in His majesty.
The eternal God is our refuge,
and underneath are the everlasting arms.
He will drive out our enemy before us,
saying, "Destroy him!"

Deuteronomy 33:25–27 (NIV)

No weapon that is formed against us shall prosper; and every tongue which rises against us in judgment we do condemn. This is our heritage as servants of the Lord, and our righteousness is from You, O Lord of hosts.

Isaiah 54:17 (KJV)*

Plead my cause, O Lord,
> with those who strive against me;
Fight against those who fight against me.
> Take hold of shield and buckler,
> And stand up for my help.
Also draw out the spear,
> And stop the way against those who pursue me.
Say to my soul,
> "I am your salvation."

Psalm 35:1–3*

Personal Prayers and Proclamations

_____

_____

_____

_____

_____

_____

_____

_____

_____

_____

_____

_____

_____

_____

_____

_____

_____

_____

_____

_____

_____

_____

_____

_____

_____

_____

_____

_____

PERFECT REDEMPTION

Now unto Him who is able to keep us from falling, and to present us faultless before the presence of His glory with exceeding joy,

To the only wise God our Saviour, be glory and majesty, dominion and power, both now and forever. Amen.

Jude 24–25 (KJV)

Bless the LORD, O my soul: and all that is within me, bless
His holy name.
Bless the LORD, O my soul, and forget not all His benefits:
Who forgiveth all thine iniquities; who healeth all thy
diseases;
Who redeemeth thy life from destruction; who crowneth
thee with lovingkindness and tender mercies;
Who satisfieth thy mouth with good things; so that thy
youth is renewed like the eagle's.

Psalm 103:1–5 (KJV)

This is our prayer:

that the God of our Lord Jesus Christ, the Father of glory, may give to us a spirit of wisdom and revelation in the knowledge of Him,

the eyes of our understanding being enlightened; that we may know what is the hope of His calling, what are the riches of the glory of His inheritance in the saints,

and what is the exceeding greatness of His power toward us who believe, according to the working of His mighty power which He worked in Christ when He raised Him from the dead and seated Him at His right hand in the heavenly places,

far above all principality and power and might and dominion, and every name that is named, not only in this age but also in that which is to come.

And He put all things under His feet, and gave Him to be head over all things to the church,

which is His body, the fullness of Him who fills all in all.

Ephesians 1:17–23

We are confident of this very thing, that He who has begun a good work in us will complete it until the day of Jesus Christ.

Philippians 1:6

For by one sacrifice He has perfected forever us who are being sanctified. Hebrews 10:14*

There is therefore now no condemnation to those who are in Christ Jesus. . . .

For the law of the Spirit of life in Christ Jesus has made me free from the law of sin and death.

Romans 8:1–2

Through the sacrifice of Jesus on the cross, I have passed out from under the curse and entered into the blessing of Abraham, whom God blessed in all things.

Based on Galatians 3:13–14
Genesis 24:1

Behold what manner of love the Father has bestowed on us, that we should be called children of God! And we are.

Therefore the world does not know us, because it did not know Him.

Beloved, now we are children of God;

and it has not yet been revealed what we shall be,

but we know that when He is revealed,

we shall be like Him, for we shall see Him as He is.

And everyone who has this hope in Him purifies

himself, just as He is pure.

1 John 3:1–3

We have known and believed the love

that God has for us.

God is love, and he who abides in love

abides in God, and God in him. 1 John 4:16

But we are washed, but we are sanctified,
but we are justified in the name of the Lord Jesus
and by the Spirit of our God.

1 Corinthians 6:11

Now may the God of peace who brought up our Lord Jesus from the dead, that great Shepherd of the sheep, through the blood of the everlasting covenant,

make us perfect in every good work to do His will,

working in us what is well pleasing in His sight, through Jesus Christ,

to whom be glory forever and ever. Amen.

Hebrews 13:20–21

Personal Prayers and Proclamations

_____

_____

_____

_____

_____

_____

_____

_____

_____

_____

_____

_____

_____

_____

_____

_____

_____

_____

_____

_____

_____

_____

_____

_____

MENTAL _and_ EMOTIONAL STABILITY

We have labored and been heavy laden, but we come to You, Lord Jesus, that You may give us rest.

We take Your yoke upon us and learn from You, for You are meek and lowly in heart, and we shall find rest for our souls.

For Your yoke is easy and Your burden is light.

Matthew 11:28–30*

There remains therefore a Sabbath-rest for the people of God.

For he who has entered His rest has himself also ceased from his works as God did from His.

Let us therefore be diligent to enter that rest, lest anyone fall after the same example of disobedience.

Hebrews 4:9–11*

You will keep me in perfect peace because my mind is
stayed on You and I trust in You.

Isaiah 26:3*

I have great peace because I love your law and nothing
shall offend me.

Psalm 119:165 (KJV)*

The weapons of my warfare are mighty in God.
With them I pull down strongholds that Satan has built in
my mind.
I bring all my thoughts into obedience to Christ.
Three of my mightiest weapons are proclamation,
thanksgiving and praise.

Based on 2 Corinthians 10:3–5

God has not given me a spirit of fear,
but of power and of love and of a sound mind.

2 Timothy 1:7

Now may the God of hope fill us with all joy and peace
in believing, that we may abound in hope by the power of
the Holy Spirit.

Romans 15:13

We are anxious for nothing, but in everything by prayer and supplication, with thanksgiving, we let our requests be made known to God;

and the peace of God, which surpasses all understanding, will guard our hearts and minds in Christ Jesus.

Finally, brethren,

> whatever things are true,
>
> whatever things are noble,
>
> whatever things are just,
>
> whatever things are pure,
>
> whatever things are lovely,
>
> whatever things are of good report,
>
> if there is any virtue,
>
> and if there is anything praiseworthy,
>
> we meditate on these things.

Philippians 4:6–8

Personal Prayers and Proclamations

_____

_____

_____

_____

_____

_____

_____

_____

_____

_____

_____

_____

_____

_____

_____

_____

_____

_____

_____

_____

_____

_____

_____

_____

_____

_____

_____

SERVING GOD

But thanks be to God, who always leads us in triumphal procession in Christ and through us spreads everywhere the fragrance of the knowledge of Him.

For we are to God the aroma of Christ among those who are being saved and those who are perishing.

To the one we are the smell of death; to the other, the fragrance of life. And who is equal to such a task?

Unlike so many, we do not peddle the word of God for profit. On the contrary, in Christ we speak before God with sincerity, like men sent from God.

2 Corinthians 2:14–17 (NIV)

God is able to do exceedingly abundantly
    above all that we ask or think,
        according to the power that works in us.

Ephesians 3:20*

God is able to make all grace abound toward us; that we, always having all suffiency in all things, may abound to every good work.

2 Corinthians 9:8 (KJV)*

Again I say to you that if two of you agree on earth concerning anything that they ask, it will be done for them by My Father in heaven.

Matthew 18:19

The harvest truly is plenteous, but the laborers are few;
Therefore we pray the Lord of the harvest, that He will thrust forth laborers into His harvest.

Matthew 9:37–38 (KJV)*

And this gospel of the kingdom will be proclaimed in all the world as a witness to all the nations, and then the end will come.

Matthew 24:14*

We will be strong and of good courage, and do it;
we will not fear nor be dismayed,
for the LORD God—our God—will be with us.
He will not leave us nor forsake us,
until we have finished all the work
for the service of the house of the LORD.

1 Chronicles 28:20

For as the rain comes down, and the snow from heaven,
> And do not return there,

But water the earth,
> And make it bring forth and bud,

That it may give seed to the sower
> And bread to the eater,

So shall My word be that goes forth from My mouth;
> It shall not return to Me void,

But it shall accomplish what I please,
> And it shall prosper in the thing for which I sent it.

Isaiah 55:10–11

We work out our own salvation with fear and trembling;
> for it is God who works in us both to will
> and to do for His good pleasure.

We do all things without grumbling and arguing,
> that we may become blameless and innocent,
> children of God without fault
> in the midst of a crooked and perverse generation,
> among whom we shine as lights in the world,
> holding forth the Word of life.

Philippians 2:12b–16a*

Let us watch, stand fast in the faith,
> be brave, be strong.

Let all that we do be done with love.

1 Corinthians 16:13–14

What things were gain to me, these I have counted loss for Christ.

But indeed I also count all things loss for the excellence of the knowledge of Christ Jesus my Lord, for whom I have suffered the loss of all things, and count them as rubbish, that I may gain Christ

and be found in Him, not having my own righteousness, which is from the law, but that which is through faith in Christ, the righteousness which is from God by faith;

that I may know Him and the power of His resurrection, and the fellowship of His sufferings, being conformed to His death,

if, by any means, I may attain to the resurrection from the dead.

Not that I have already attained, or am already perfected; but I press on, that I may lay hold of that for which Christ Jesus has also laid hold of me.

Brethren, I do not count myself to have apprehended; but one thing I do, forgetting those things which are behind and reaching forward to those things which are ahead,

I press toward the goal for the prize of the upward call of God in Christ Jesus.

Philippians 3:7–14

But you, O man of God, flee these things
>   and pursue righteousness, godliness, faith,
>   love, patience, gentleness.
>   Fight the good fight of the faith, lay hold on eternal life,
>   to which you were also called and have confessed the
good confession in the presence of many witnesses.
>   I urge you in the sight of God who gives life to all
things,
>   and before Christ Jesus who witnessed the good con-
fession before Pontius Pilate,
>   that you keep this command without spot,
>   blameless until our Lord Jesus Christ's appearing,
>   which He will manifest in His own time,
He who is the blessed and only Potentate,
>   the King of kings and Lord of lords,
>   who alone has immortality,
>   dwelling in unapproachable light,
>   whom no man has seen or can see,
>   to whom be honor and everlasting power. Amen.

1 Timothy 6:11–16

"Now the just shall live by faith;
But if anyone draws back,
My soul has no pleasure in him."

But we are not of those who draw back to perdition,
>   but of those who believe to the saving of the soul.

Hebrews 10:38–39*

91

If then we were raised with Christ,

> we seek those things which are above,

> where Christ is, sitting at the right hand of God.

We set our minds on things above,

> not on things on the earth.

For we died, and our life is hidden

> with Christ in God.

When Christ who is our life appears,

> then we also will appear with Him in glory.

Colossians 3:1–4

I have been crucified with Christ;

> it is no longer I who live, but Christ lives in me;

and the life which I now live in the flesh

> I live by the faith in the Son of God,

> who loved me

> and gave Himself for me.

Galatians 2:20*

Personal Prayers and Proclamations

_____

_____

_____

_____

_____

_____

_____

_____

_____

_____

_____

_____

_____

_____

_____

_____

_____

_____

_____

_____

_____

_____

_____

_____

_____

_____

THE EXCHANGE MADE *at the* CROSS

Jesus was **punished**
   that we might be **forgiven**.[5]

Jesus was **wounded**
   that we might be **healed**.[6]

Jesus was made **sin with our sinfulness**
   that we might be
   made **righteous with His righteousness**.[7]

Jesus died our **death**
   that we might receive His **life**.[8]

Jesus was made a **curse**
   that we might enter into the **blessing**.[9]

Jesus endured our **poverty**
   that we might share His **abundance**.[10]

Jesus bore our **shame**
   that we might share His **glory**.[11]

Jesus endured our **rejection**
   that we might have His **acceptance** with the Father.[12]

Jesus was **cut off** by death
   that we might be **joined** to God eternally.[13]

Our **old man** was put to death in Him
   that the **new man** might come to life in us.[14]

LET THE REDEEMED SAY SO[15]

My body is a temple for the Holy Spirit[16], redeemed[17], cleansed[18], and sanctified by the blood of Jesus.[19]

My members, the parts of my body, are instruments of righteousness[20], yielded to God for His service and for His glory.

The devil has no place in me, no power over me, no unsettled claims against me.

All has been settled by the blood of Jesus.[21]

I overcome Satan by the blood of the Lamb and by the word of my testimony, and I do not love my life to the death.[22]

My body is for the Lord and the Lord is for my body.[23]

NOTHING
but the
BLOOD

We overcome Satan when we testify personally to what the Word of God says the blood of Jesus does for us.[24]

Through the blood of Jesus,
    I am redeemed out of the hand of the devil.[25]

Through the blood of Jesus, all my sins are forgiven.[26]

Through the blood of Jesus,
    I am continually being cleansed from all sin.[27]

Through the blood of Jesus,
    I am justified, made righteous, just-as-if-I'd never sinned.[28]

Through the blood of Jesus,
    I am sanctified, made holy, set apart to God.[29]

Through the blood of Jesus,
    I have boldness to enter into the presence of God.[30]

The blood of Jesus cries out continually
    to God in heaven on my behalf.[31]

DECLARATION
of CONFIDENCE *in*
GOD'S PROTECTION

No weapon that is formed against me shall prosper and every tongue that arises against me in judgment I do condemn. This is my heritage as a servant of the Lord and my righteousness is from You, O Lord of Hosts.

If there are those who have been speaking or praying against me, or seeking to harm me, or who have rejected me, I forgive them (name people if you know them). Having forgiven them, I bless them in the name of the Lord.[32]

Now I declare, O Lord, that You and You alone are my God and beside You there is no other; a just God and a Savior, the Father, the Son and the Spirit, and I worship You! I submit myself afresh to You today in unreserved obedience.

Having submitted to You, Lord, I do as Your Word directs. I resist the devil: all his pressures, his attacks, his deceptions and every instrument or agent he would seek to use against me. I do not submit! I resist him, drive him from me and exclude him from me in Jesus' name.

Specifically I reject and repel: infirmity, infection, pain, inflammation, malignancies, allergies, viruses, every form of witchcraft and every type of stress (name any sickness or spirit that you feel has been coming against you).

Finally, Lord, I thank You that through the sacrifice of Jesus on the cross, I have passed out from under the curse and entered into the blessings of Abraham whom You blessed in all things: exaltation, health, reproductiveness, prosperity, victory, God's favor and God's friendship.[33]

Amen.

FOOTNOTES:

[1] See Matthew 5:43–45; Romans 12:14

[2] Name any sickness or spirits that you feel have been coming against you.

[3] See Galatians 3:13–14; Genesis 24:1

[4] Direct translation from the original Greek

[5] Isaiah 53:4–5

[6] Isaiah 53:4–5

[7] Isaiah 53:10; 2 Corinthians 5:21

[8] Hebrews 2:9

[9] Galatians 3:13–14

[10] 2 Corinthians 8:9, 9:8

[11] Matthew 27:35–36; Hebrews 12:2, 2:9

[12] Matthew 27:46–51; Ephesians 1:5–6

[13] Isaiah 53:8; 1 Corinthians 6:17

[14] Romans 6:6; Colossians 3:9–10

[15] Psalm 107:2

[16] 1 Corinthians 6:19

[17] Ephesians 1:7

[18] 1 John 1:7

[19] Hebrews 13:12

[20] Romans 6:13

[21] Romans 3:23–25, 8:33–34

[22] Revelation 12:11

[23] 1 Corinthians 6:13

[24] Revelation 12:11

[25] Ephesians 1:7

[26] 1 John 1:9

[27] 1 John 1:7

[28] Romans 5:9

[29] Hebrews 13:12

[30] Hebrews 10:19

[31] Hebrews 12:24

[32] See Matthew 5:43–45; Romans 12:14

[33] See Galatians 3:13–14; Genesis 24:1

SCRIPTURE INDEX

ABOUT
the
AUTHOR

Derek Prince (1915–2003) was born in India of British parents. Educated as a scholar of Greek and Latin at Eton College and Cambridge University, England, he held a Fellowship in Ancient and Modern Philosophy at King's College. He also studied several modern languages, including Hebrew and Aramaic, at Cambridge University and the Hebrew University in Jerusalem.

While serving with the British army in World War II, he began to study the Bible and experienced a life-changing encounter with Jesus Christ. Out of this encounter he formed two conclusions: first, that Jesus Christ is alive; second, that the Bible is a true, relevant, up-to-date book. These conclusions altered the whole course of his life, which he then devoted to studying and teaching the Bible.

Derek's main gift of explaining the Bible and its teaching in a clear and simple way has helped build a foundation of faith in millions of lives. His non-denominational, non-sectarian approach has made his teaching equally relevant and helpful to people from all racial and religious backgrounds.

He is the author of over 50 books, 500 audio and 140 video teachings, many of which have been translated and published in more than 60 languages. His daily radio broadcast, Derek Prince Legacy Radio, is translated into Arabic, Chinese (Amoy, Cantonese, Mandarin, Shanghaiese, Swatow), Croatian, German, Malagasy, Mongolian, Russian, Samoan, Spanish and Tongan. The radio program continues to touch lives around the world.

B69/0107